I0409892

Contents

Paper Abstract

An Argument for Consolidation: The ANZUS Carrier Task Force

The ANZUS (Australia – New Zealand – United States) Treaty has evolved into a series of strong, individually bipartisan relationships. ANZUS Naval cooperation is a gold standard to which other alliances aspire. A recent shift in strategic attention to the Indo-Pacific region, the challenges posed by the Indo-Pacific, and financial restrictions on defense expenditures are shared concerns of each ANZUS nation, and are directly addressed within their overlapping national strategies. One possible solution to the complex problem, multi-faceted problem of threats and challenges within the Indo-Pacific is the US Navy Carrier Strike Group (CSG), but CSG's can be encumbered either by geographic factors related to world's oceans or threatening regional military systems. To adequately address the shared challenges of Indo-Pacific maritime threats, defense restrictions, and geographic limitations; a consolidated, integrated, and forward-deployed multi-national maritime Carrier Task Force ought to be established at Fleet-Base West in Perth, Australia: The ANZUS Carrier Task Force.

Introduction

The *Indo-Pacific (IP)* poses a myriad of 21st century challenges for operational

planners. Maritime choke points bordered by nations saddled with a host of concerns,

compounded with global recession and rising defense costs, have led to a dramatic shift

global strategy and security attention. *Cooperative Strategy for the 21st Century* asserts that

"global maritime partnerships are essential in preventing disruptions and containing

conflict."[1] In this complex environment, the U.S. and its allies are faced with a challenge to

accomplish more, with less, and find feasible, aligned, cooperative, and effective solutions

that provide adequate, persistent maritime presence.

ANZUS (1951) is a Cold-War era defense treaty among Australia (AUS), New

Zealand (NZ), and the U.S. designed to counter communism and provide strategic assurance.

Since its inception, it has evolved into a diplomatic tool for bilateral partnership and military

support.[2] AUS and the U.S. maintain strong ties; a brotherly relationship of dependency

bonds AUS and NZ. Additionally, the U.S. and NZ are increasing military cooperation after

recent diplomatic compromise.[3] Sharing heritage and language, values and principles,

respect and appreciation, all forged through World War; *the idea* of ANZUS remains a

promising avenue for increased cooperation and continues to be model for military alliances,

markedly between the U.S. Navy (USN) and Royal Australian Navy (RAN).

While "Constrained budgets and transitions make this a challenging era for maritime

forces,"[4] the U.S. Navy Carrier Strike Group (CSG) represents a real, ready, flexible, and

credible solution to the full spectrum of threats inside the *IP*. Able to transit vast oceans on

short notice to both promote goodwill and protect national interests; the CSG is a *globally recognized* symbol of U.S. commitment and resolve.[5] However, CSG's are saddled with the finite geographic factors of deploying from North America. Therefore, the U.S. must do as the CSG does: adapt.

Shared challenges have shifted ANZUS priorities, requiring a cooperative solution. The *IP* warrants a "forward-deployed maritime presence"[6] capable of combating the full-spectrum of maritime concerns and an increased maritime presence. A CSG is capable of providing this, but must overcome *time-space-force* factors that limit it. These compounded drivers require ANZUS to do more, with less, in the face of growing challenges. ANZUS' operational familiarity and overlapping capabilities are cause for consolidation. **Therefore, AUS, NZ, and the U.S. should align and establish a permanent, forward-deployed, multilateral, and *operational* command at *Fleet-Base West* in Perth, Australia: *The ANZUS Carrier Task Force* (CTF-ANZUS).**

Shared Challenges

Part of the problem is that this shift in focus is coupled with a change in supply and demand. Addressing the Australian Parliament in November 2011, U.S. President Barack Obama asserted, "As we end today's wars, I have directed my national security team to make our presence and mission in Asia-Pacific a top priority...reductions in U.S. defense spending will not- I repeat, *will not* - come at the expense of the Asia-Pacific."[7] This *"Pacific Pivot,"* a concentrated shift to the *IP,*[8] is due to its growing importance and the need to provide it with *core naval capabilities* of "Forward Presence, Maritime Security Operations (MSO), Humanitarian Assistance and Disaster Response (HA/DR), Sea Control, Power Projection, and Deterrence."[9]

Within the *IP,* defined as the East / West expanse from the Gulf of Aden to Wake Island and the North / South expanse from Japan to American Samoa, are critical linkages in the global economy atop 22.5 million square nautical miles. One-half of oil exports move by tankers on fixed maritime routes,[10] 20% of the world's oil flows through the Strait of Hormuz and 40% of the world's trade passes through the Strait of Malacca.[11] These 'chokepoints' leave shipping vulnerable to piracy, terrorism, hostile political unrest, and instability; and their geographic location within the *IP,* a region with an infamous history of natural disasters on a grand scale, increase their fragility. While natural and man-made disasters, crime, and violence can and will occur in the future, ANZUS must be resolute in preparing accordingly to meet these threats while building on shared historical success.

A third challenge exists in Iran, North Korea (DPRK), and the expanding military influence of China (PRC). Countering Iranian threats of regional war and closure of the

Strait of Hormuz and providing persistent deterrence to a hazardous DPRK posture have been shared ANZUS naval challenges since the end of the Korean War. The responsibility of providing assured freedom of the seas for uninterrupted commerce is inherent in each ANZUS national strategy. As these resolute threats are attached to the maritime domain, ANZUS navies must be prepared and accordingly postured to provide a persistent and credible deterrence to a two-ocean problem, as these threats (Iran - PRC & DPRK) are separated by 6,000 nautical miles (nm). While ANZUS, like the UN, desires to avoid armed conflict with other nations while both preserving and protecting the global commons, the need to provide a credible deterrence necessary for diplomacy to run its course is an important part of both AUS and US *naval* strategies and doctrine.

While ANZUS maintains a presence in the Persian Gulf and continually provide deterrence against Iranian aggressive action, U.S. Forward-Deployed Naval Forces (FDNF) in Bahrain and Jebel-Ali are within range of Iranian weapons. An even a greater concern considers the PRC, for while diplomatic engagement and the desire to foster a strong working relationship[12] with the PRC is a shared ANZUS approach, FDNF in Japan, Korea, the Philippines, Guam, and Singapore are all within PRC or DPRK ballistic and anti-ship missile ranges. Given the capacity of PRC surface and submarine assets to extend this further, AUS and NZ can expect to become increasingly within range of the PRC Anti-Access / Area-Denial (A2D2) weapons.[13] To adequately and wholly counter these shared concerns and threats, a multi-lateral force built on familiarity, trust, and a tradition of excellence exemplified in the history of ANZUS is required.

ANZUS History

An historical background must be established in order to propose a combined ANZUS solution. To begin, ANZUS' naval *origins* date back to 1908, when AUS Prime Minister Alfred Deakin, influenced by Captain William Creswell of the Royal Navy (RN) and visits by the USN's "Great White Fleet," lobbied (unsuccessfully) for U.S. Pacific-extension of the Monroe Doctrine but successfully procured the first ships for the newly created RAN.[14] Naval *cooperation* can be traced to the ANZAC Squadron, an allied command of RAN, RNZN, and USN warships established in 1942 and dedicated to the Commonwealth defense from Imperial Japan. Under operational direction of Task-Force 44's RADM John Crace (RN), TF-44 significantly contributed in the Battle of the Coral Sea.[15] Ever since the Battle of the Coral Sea, ANZUS naval cooperation has been evident in nearly every major conflict.

In the Korean War the RAN served with NATO, supporting USN blockading, patrol and logistical missions. In the Vietnam War the RAN was part of the 'Gun Line' alongside USN destroyers, providing naval gunfire support against North Vietnamese targets. During the Cold War the RAN routinely contributed warships, including the aircraft carrier *HMAS Melbourne*, towards regional security through Southeast Asia Treaty Organization (SEATO) in Exercise *SEA DEVIL,*[16] working with the USN and RNZN in the process. In the Gulf War, the RAN assisted the coalition by providing Maritime Security Operations (MSO) in Operation *DAMASK*.[17] Since 9/11, the RAN has been a stalwart teammate of the USN, assisting U.S. and NATO forces in Operation *SLIPPER*[18] by providing MSO (including counter piracy and counter-terrorism) as part of the Combined Maritime Forces (CMF) under

5th Fleet Command. RAN officers command Combined Task Forces (CTF) such as CTF-150, directing MSO missions of 25 nations in the Gulf of Aden.[19] RAN-USN familiarity is perhaps best displayed through the biennial Exercise *TALISMAN SABRE (TS)*, held exclusively between the Australian Defense Force (ADF) and the U.S. *TS* represents the "closeness of our reliance and the strength of our military-military relationship"[20] and increases the combat readiness of the RAN and USN. In *TS* 2010, interoperability was exhibited when an RAN officer commanded a USN-RAN amphibious task force.[21]

The RNZN has a similar history of cooperation with the U.S. and AUS. Also attached to the ANZAC Squadron in WWII; throughout the Korean War the RNZN committed two *Loch-class* frigates to the NATO mission where it routinely supported USN efforts by providing naval gunfire support and coastal patrols. While NZ participation in Vietnam War was land-based, throughout much of Cold War naval cooperation continued through SEATO exercises and *RIMPAC* (Rim of the Pacific).[22] The mid-1980s rift between the U.S. and NZ over nuclear power and weaponry, as NZ banned any nuclear-powered or nuclear-armed ships from NZ ports, led to a decrease in naval cooperation.[23] In 1986, the U.S. rescinded its NZ-ANZUS commitments, relations declined, and the RNZN ceased to participate in *RIMPAC.*[24] Diplomatic compromise after 9/11 has helped renew USN and RNZN cooperation and the RNZN operates with USN forces today, providing MSO as part of the CMF. The most promising symbol of future USN-RNZN cooperation stems from the November 2010 Wellington Declaration, "which affirms a new strategic partnership between the U.S. and NZ," and the April 2011 announcement that the RNZN will resume participation in *RIMPAC* 2012.[25]

Tripartite cooperation is exhibited in Operation *Pacific Partnership* and *RIMPAC*. *Pacific Partnership,* a goodwill mission of ANZUS and other allied nations in providing HA/DR to neighboring Pacific island nations exemplifies the shared commitment ANZUS has to *IP* stability.[26] *RIMPAC*; the world's largest multi-national naval exercise, where the RAN has been a participant since its 1971 inception and as previously mentioned where the RNZN will resume participation in 2012, greatly expands combat interoperability between all participants by identifying and bridging gaps through tactical and operational maritime planning and training.[27] While cooperation between ANZUS will cement partnerships, the support and commitment of each nation would be based on their individual strategies and capabilities.

Strategic Overlap

Strategic overlap provides a framework for consolidation. For the U.S., balancing 21st century strategies and budgets will be a daunting task as seen in both the U.S. 2012 Strategy Review and associated Fiscal Year 2013 (FY13) Defense Budget. Remarking on the FY13 budget, U.S. Secretary of Defense Leon Panetta articulates the need for a "smaller, leaner, agile, and flexible force; the need to rebalance and globally posture in order to emphasize Asia-Pacific and the Middle East; to foster partnerships and strengthen key alliances; and to confront and defeat aggression from any adversary, anywhere, and protect and prioritize the capacity to grow."[28] Fortunately, USN budgets have been protected as attention towards the maritime domain expands, and this expanded naval strategy lies intrinsically with AUS.[29] U.S. Secretary of State Hillary Clinton argues for "strengthening bilateral security alliances, engaging with multilateral institutions…and forging a broad-based military presence." She further asserts that these challenges stretch across the *IP,* and that the solution lies directly with U.S. presence and AUS cooperation, saying "We our expanding our alliance with AUS from a Pacific Partnership to an Indo-Pacific one."[30]

Australian strategy is similar in its view not only of the *IP,* but the role the U.S. plays within it. Not only is AUS strategically aligned with the U.S., but the 2010 Defense Trade Cooperation means that "approximately 50% of AUS war-fighting assets are sourced from the U.S."[31] AUS's 2009 Defence (sic) White Paper is the driver behind AUS defence planning and has fed into the March 2012 Force Posture Review (FPR), both planning around a force in 2030. These address the need for the U.S. and AUS to be postured correctly and cooperatively engaged in the *IP* while acknowledging an expanding PRC influence and the need to counter-balance that influence. It also addresses fragile conditions that could adversely affect the *IP,* and that these warrant immediate U.S. and AUS attention and dedicated force application. The White Paper asserts that "Australia's strategic outlook over the coming decades will continue to be shaped by the changing global distribution of economic, political and military power, and by the future role and weight of the U.S."[32] It further states how these challenges require *maritime* solutions. "Balancing the capabilities required for unconventional operations… while retaining high-tech conventional forces, will be a challenge for U.S. defence planners, and the U.S. will seek further deepening of its strategic relationships with coalition partners, such as Australia."

The U.S. and AUS recognize that "Keeping the U.S. engaged in Asia has been and continues to be a key foreign policy objective of AUS." [33] At AUSMIN 2010 (AUS-US Ministerial Consultations), the principal forum for bilateral consultations, a US-AUS Force Posture Working Group was established to examine options for enhancing defence cooperation, increased training, port visits, HA/DR cooperation and a greater U.S. presence in AUS.[34] This led to the November 2011 announcement of a 2,500 U.S. Marine detachment in Darwin, AUS and increased access to RAAF (AUS Air Force) Bases in the north (AUS).[35] At AUSMIN 2011, historic in that it marked both the 60-year ANZUS anniversary and the 10 years since the AUS enactment after 9/11, Panetta issued a pointed assertion, echoed by his AUS counterpart Defence Minister Stephen Smith, "to strengthen the relationship and send a clear signal to the Asia-Pacific region that the U.S. and AUS are going to make very clear to those that would threaten us that we are going to stick together."[36] The drawdown of U.S. and AUS forces in Iraq and Afghanistan along with increasingly shared economic and security interests, led Panetta to further assert that these factors "merit an assessment of U.S.

defensive strategy in light of the changing geopolitical environment and our changing fiscal circumstances." He further states that out of necessity, the U.S. must rebalance towards the *IP* and place a premium on U.S. and allied continued, persistent military presence.[37]

New Zealand defense strategy is similar to AUS and the U.S. in its assessment of the importance and fragility of the *IP* and the competing influence between the U.S. and PRC, but different in that it recognizes its smaller capacity and dependency on AUS and the U.S. "The cost of the capabilities required to contribute to high-end combat between large and sophisticated military forces is increasingly beyond our means."[38] The 2010 Defence White Paper serves as the NZ centerpiece for future defense and recognizes that "AUS is our principal defence and security partner." It highlights the NZ requirement to respond to any direct attack on AUS and that NZ security is enhanced by the investment AUS has made in its national defence. Stating further, "AUS has military capabilities that we do not have, but which are essential for higher-end contingencies."[39]

It recognizes that the ANZAC (AUS-NZ) relationship enhances the depth and reaches of NZ and adds to its strategic weight, but that it will also benefit from being an engaged, active, and stalwart partner of the U.S. NZ acknowledges that because of its limited means it must get the most out its smaller defense forces, particularly the RNZN, as NZ strategic concerns are heavily dominated by the immediate maritime domain. Finally, it asserts that it will always need an adequate force to participate and contribute to regional security, supporting "coalition efforts where possible, and cooperative defence with AUS."[40]

The Carrier Strike Group

It is possible to implement these overlapping strategies while simultaneously strengthening national ties and interoperability, all while consolidating cost savings through one unrivaled and multipurpose platform: *Nimitz*-class Aircraft Carriers (CVN) and their associated CSGs. The complex problems of the *IP* require that the aforementioned challenges be met with a cohesive, interoperable force capable of providing "full utility across the spectrum of military operations from peace operations to combat operations."[41] This force exists in a CSG.

As an HA/DR asset after the 2004 Indonesian Tsunami, USS Abraham Lincoln became a 'Lilly Pad' for helicopter rescue operations, saving hundreds of victims stranded off shore and inland while providing a lifeline of supplies. The Carrier Air Wing (CVW) E-2C Hawkeye's provided rescue coordination through airborne command and control while C-2 logistical aircraft transported victims to shore based medical facilities. The onboard berthing, medical facilities, food supply, and ability to produce 200,000 gallons of drinking water meant the CVN had become a floating haven. Less than five weeks after the disaster happened "USS Lincoln had delivered over 4.8 million lbs. of relief supplies."[42] CVN-based HA/DR efforts were also evident in the aftermath of the 2010 Haiti earthquake in *Operation UNIFIED RESPONSE*[43] and in Japan in 2011 in support of *Operation TOMODACHI.*[44]

As a combat asset, a CSG can rapidly deploy CVW aircraft to interdict targets at sea or far inland, as was the case in *Operation ENDURING FREEDOM (OEF)*[45] and *Operation IRAQI FREEDOM,* while the attached DESRON (Destroyer Squadron) can conduct MSO, establish Sea Control, or project power ashore with naval guns and Tomahawk Land Attack

Missiles (TLAMs), as seen in 2011 in Libya during *Operation ODYSSEY DAWN.* CSG's also have the flexibility to support joint amphibious operations, as was the case in the 1994 *Operation UPHOLD DEMOCRACY,* when USS Eisenhower (CVN-69) transported elements of the U.S. Army 10th Mountain Division into Haiti to conduct forced entry operations.[46] Perhaps the greatest example of CSG flexibility and reach was exemplified by the Royal Navy in the 1982 Falklands War, where HMS *Hermes* and *Invincible* traversed over 12,000 miles in one month to conduct combat operations. Finally, the presence of CSG's provides strong deterrence and demonstrates resolve to would-be adversaries.

The principle challenge for CSGs, as seen in the Falklands War, is often the *time and space* limitations created by the world's oceans and the finite distances they represent. A CSG home-ported in San Diego is 5,500 nm from Guam, located on the far western fringe of the *IP*, has another 2,500 nm to the southern entrance of the Strait of Malacca. A Norfolk-based CSG is 6,700 nm from the Gulf of Aden, located on the far Western fringe of the *IP* and has another 3,300 nm to the Strait of Malacca. For either to rapidly deploy to the *IP* requires approximately 12 days of uninterrupted transit at 25kts. Factor in time to mobilize, load material, transit to sea, 'fly-on' the CVW, and conduct en-route flight operations and underway replenishment; the actual time required for a CSG, from receiving a stateside deployment order to conducting operations in the *IP*, easily exceeds three weeks. A transit and eventual return to the continental homeport requires approximately 15,000 nm and one month alone to be spent purely on *transit time vs. operational time* (*operational time* meaning time spent conducting operations and providing a presence).

In 2011, the USN executed seven CSG west coast and two east coast deployments.[47] Given that each CSG traveled at least to the *IP*, it conservatively amounts to approximately nine months and 135,000 nm of CSG transit time. Put in even broader time terms: In 2011 CSGs collectively spent the time required for two full 4.5-month deployments purely on oceanic transit.

Positioned correctly, forward-deployed CSGs minimize this gap through continued presence. Currently, the only permanently forward-deployed CSG is CSG-5 in Yokosuka, Japan. Providing a credible presence and supporting allied partners (Japan, South Korea, Philippines), it invaluably serves Pacific Command (PACOM) and the USN 7th Fleet as a 24-hour on call combat source and is "an average of 17 steaming days closer to locations in Asia than naval forces based in the continental U.S."[48] For example, USS Kitty Hawk (CV-63) rapidly transited to project power ashore in the early stages of OEF in 2001 while also providing regional assurance to South Korea through exercise *Invincible Spirit*. CSG-5 is often used by PACOM for partnered international cooperation, such as *RIMPAC*.

The only unbridgeable gap it can never close is, once again, that of *time and space*, for Yokosuka is on the far Northeastern Asian fringe of the *IP* and is over 6,500 nm from the Gulf of Aden; as far as a Norfolk CSG. With this in mind, ANZUS planners would have greater options and reach with a CSG that is more centrally postured inside the *IP*. While geographic restrictions on both continentally-based CSG's and CSG-5 have been founded, CSG-5 is also at a strategic disadvantage. Yokosuka is within range of both DPRK missiles and submarine patrols and, considering the advancing PRC A2/D2 surface, submarine, missile threat; CSG-5 is now susceptible to crippling attack and the loss of deterrence. These geographic and strategic limitations on CSG-5 infer that it is not adequately postured for 21st Century *IP* maritime challenges. Perth, located outside most estimated PRC envelopes, would be a centrally located safe haven within the IP by safeguarding a CSG from the

14

aforementioned threats while in homeport yet providing easy access once underway. Figure 1 below displays how the current estimated range of the PRC's land-based DF-21D Anti-Surface Ballistic Cruise Missile (ASBM), designed to (and capable of) "attacking aircraft carriers, other U.S. Navy ships, or ships of allied or partner navies operating in the Western Pacific"[49] while they are underway by using satellite terminal guidance, has an estimated range of over 1,500 (possibly out to 2,500 kilometers in the coming years).

This system envelopes FDNF's in Japan and Korea, and further development will likely see it reach to FDNF's in Singapore and Guam in the near term. However robust it is, as of now it is limited in reach beyond the "2nd Island Chain" of the PRC's A2/D2 system[51] and falls far short of Fleet Base West (*FBW*), located on the southwest tip of Australia. While "China is capable of targeting its nuclear forces throughout the region and most of the world, including the continental United States,"[52] their proximity of Perth renders it protected from a bulk of PRC missile ranges. Figure 2 below, taken from the 2011 US Department of Defense report on the Military and Security Developments Involving the PRC, shows how Perth, and as of now all of Australia, is geographically protected from the A2/D2 system that envelopes much of the water inside the *IP*.

Integration

If history instills confidence in cooperation and challenges align strategies, the addition of CSG time-space restrictions merits forward posturing and consolidation. For the RAN, maintaining a continued presence in the Middle East via CMF participation while also adequately maintaining an Asia-Pacific presence will be difficult as the operational reach it will be required to address encompasses such a vast amount of ocean. As an island nation affixed to the *IP* the RAN "faces the greatest challenge in accommodating changes required by Force 2030."[54] The AUS White Paper aims for the ADF to "establish and maintain sea control and air superiority at key locations in the ADF's primary operational environment; project maritime and air power beyond that area if that is necessary in order to defend Australia; and maintain awareness of our sea and air approaches."[55]

The RAAF and RAN are expanding to meet these demands. From 2014-15 the RAN will introduce three *Hobart*-class Air Warfare Destroyers (AWD) and add two *Canberra*-class Amphibious Assault ships (LHD) to its surface fleet.[56] The LHD's will be the largest ships ever operated by the RAN while AWD's will be the most advanced platform; equipped with the advanced *Aegis* radar and capable of "operating across the full spectrum of joint naval operations.[57]" In the longer term, the fleet of *Anzac*-class and *Adelaide*-class frigates, as well as coastal patrol boats, mine-hunters and heavy landing craft will all be replaced with larger and more capable platforms.[58] Finally, the *Collins*-class submarines of the RAN will be replaced with the "Future Submarine."

RNZN naval strategy is based upon upgrades to its two *Anzac*-class frigates, their associated SH-2G Seasprite Helicopters, modifications to its amphibious ship HMNZS

Canterbury, and additional upgrades to its fleet of six land-based AP-3. Many of these have recently participated in operations with USN CSGs and could likely fill roles in CSG integration.[59] Furthermore, a large portion of the RNZN is dedicated to its role in the ANZAC Ready Response Force (RRF), an arrangement to jointly cooperate in response to regional HA/DR contingencies. It is in the RRF where a noticeable gap appears. The RAN has a shortage in amphibious ship availability. While it is working to bridge this gap through the recent purchase of the support vessel MSV *Skandi Bergen*, its future *Canberra*-class ships will not be operational for some time.[60] This HA/DR gap is compounded by recent troubles of NZ's HMNZS *Canterbury*,[61] the principal amphibious ship in the RNZN. These shortcomings were evident after both Cyclone Yasi and the Christchurch Earthquake in 2011.[62] The USN could help alleviate this HA/DR gap through a credible, on-call HA/DR presence such as a CSG.

When taken together, the above evidence provides an optimistic view of future ANZAC naval options, but also shared needs; and it further provides a promising outlook for AUS and NZ integration with a CSG. The proven deployments of *Anzac* and *Adelaide* frigates with both CMF operations and in RIMPAC make them likely candidates. While the *Hobart*-class has yet to be delivered to the RAN, *Hobart* integration with a CSG has already been successfully proven after the integration of the Spanish *Alvaro de Bazan*, which fully integrated with the USS Theodore Roosevelt CSG in 2005.[63] The *Hobart*-class is a Spanish-produced ship and identical to the *Alvaro de Bazan*.[64] Additionally, the RAN is upgrading its maritime air capacity with the MH-60R (Naval Combat Helicopter) along with upgrades in shore-based maritime air from the AP-3 to the P-8. For the RNZN, a proven history of

18

operating its *Anzac*-class FFGs as part of the CMF and periodically with CSGs offers evidence of possible interoperability.[65]

The AUS White Paper intends for the RAAF to address "air and sea elements;" an ambitious goal considering AUS's lack of an aircraft carrier. One area of concern lies with the RAAF Joint Strike Fighter (JSF), as current delivery delays have caused AUS to initiate a review of their JSF program. To ease this shortfall, the RAAF purchased 24 F/A-18F Super Hornets, the very same CVN-based strike aircraft flown by the USN.[66] Additionally, all RAAF F/A-18F aircrew and maintenance personnel were initially trained at Naval Air Station Lemoore, CA under the instruction of USN aircrew and maintainers and Boeing contractors. While the RAAF has flown "legacy" F/A-18A's for decades, it was never equipped for CVN operations. The F/A-18F however, could be configured for CVN operations and in 2007 a RAAF exchange pilot successfully completed aircraft carrier qualifications.[67]

The MH-60R, AP-3, P-8A, and F/A-18F are nearly identical to their USN counterparts and the RAN ability to operate surface ships and helicopters with the USN has long since been proven,[68] as have RAN AP-3 maritime patrols in support of CSGs. Given that the RAN flew off HMAS *Melbourne* in previous generations and in light of RAAF Pilots success in F/A-18F training, the possibility exists for RAAF F/A-18F's to fly off of CVNs.

Posturing

The planned posturing of US assets within the *IP* has begun as USMC rotations and RAAF airfield usage by U.S. military aircraft are already in progress.[69] In the coming months the USN will stage four Littoral Combat Ships (LCS) in Singapore while replacing minesweeper ships in Bahrain with the more capable LCS's, both with the intent of increasing MSO and access in the Straits of Malacca and Hormuz.[70] Initial budget and planning stages for the development of a deep-draft wharf for transient CVNs in Guam, as well as the proposed repositioning of USMC personnel to Guam, are under Congressional review.[71] Despite these new additions the on-call strength of 7th Fleet remains in Yokosuka, but the "more broadly distributed" sentiments of President Obama would infer that the true *Pacific Pivot* lies "in the increasingly vital southern part of (Asia) on the basis of a much more flexible model than Northeast Asia."[72]

AUS Defence Minister Stephen Smith has remarked about the possible expansion of *Fleet-Base West (FBW)*, the primary RAN base in West Australia. These remarks have gained even further traction in 2012 as the precise *recommendations* of the FPR.

> "Defence should develop options to expand wharf capacity and support facilities at Fleet Base West to support major surface combatant capability and operations by providing adequate infrastructure and facilities, including missile loading and maintenance facilities, to homeport the Future Frigate class and forward deploy at least one Air Warfare Destroyer **and ensure such facilities are also able to be used for deployments and operations in Southeast Asia and the Indian Ocean by USN major surface combatants and aircraft carriers**; support submarine capability and operations by enabling FBW to continue as the primary submarine homeport when the expanded Future Submarine fleet enters service; and ensuring such facilities are also able to be used by USN submarines."[73]

This answers two of the most daunting questions concerning the posturing of a 2nd FDNF CSG: *Who would be willing to allow it? Where would you physically put it?*

Expansion of *FBW* wharf capacity and support facilities to support major surface combatant capability "for deployments and operations in Southeast Asia and the Indian Ocean by U.S. Navy major surface combatants and aircraft carriers"[74] should be welcome news for USN leadership. Challenges in permanently basing a 2nd forward-deployed CVN anywhere in the world are steep, but *FBW* represents a feasible solution. The geographic arguments for doing so are simple: the distance from *FBW* - Jakarta, Indonesia (a critical economic center located in the heart of the *IP*) is less than 1,900 nm. Additionally, *transit time* to and from Jakarta is entirely *operational time*, as that space is all within the *IP*. *FBW* could be seen as a THE "*Pacific Pivot*" point, as it is nearly 4,700 nm (by sea) from both the Strait of Hormuz *and* Tokyo. Its southern location and considerable distance from mainland PRC A2/AD systems provide it a geographic haven yet its relative proximity to Jakarta increases *IP* accessibility. Figure 3 below shows the idle proximity of *FBW* and the quick access approaches it has to the most critical parts of the *IP*. Each red line leading out of *FBW* is approximately 4700nm and 7.5 days of travel at the CSG standard of 25kts.

To translate its attractiveness to ANZUS operational planners, a CSG stationed at *FBW* could sortie and conduct MSO or HA/DR off any part East Africa, provide a forward presence off the coast of Iran, or conduct goodwill training with the small navies of Micronesia and Samoa. Furthermore, it could each of those without being within range of A2/D2 weapons. If necessary, it could venture into the A2/D2 coverage and conduct operations in the Strait of Malacca in less than 3 days, or even provide deterrence off the coast of North Korea or make a port call in Japan within the 7.5 days mentioned previously. Put bluntly, the emergency rapid response time for a CSG is reduced drastically.

While the FPR points out and identifies the need for increased pier infrastructure, upgrades in ship berthing, and overall expansion of *FBW*, it also includes recommendation for expansion and upgrades to *Fleet-Base East* (Sydney), AND other RAN locations would be necessary to ease the strain on any one port. Home-port dispersion of surface units amongst *FBW, FBE*, Guam, and Devonport (RNZN) would help ease this expansion requirement. Having a CSG heavily dispersed across a region while in home port is not a new concept, as east and west-coast CSGs are drawn from CVNs, DESRONs, CVWs, and Submarines located across multiple bases in California, Washington, Virginia, Georgia, and Florida, and Hawaii.

For the CVW, RAAF bases Amberly or Williamtown would likely require expansion, but sharing type-model aircraft (F/A-18C/F, MH-60R, P-8, KC-130) would enable consolidated maintenance, and the aforementioned familiarity and also shared physical security concerns makes this a possibility.

> "Defence should upgrade... Edinburgh, Learmonth, Pearce, Tindal and Townsville to enable unrestricted operations by KC-30 and P-8 aircraft, noting that Darwin already meets these criteria and Curtin is a lower priority for upgrade. Defence should upgrade Curtin, Learmonth, Tindal and Townsville, with Scherger as a lower priority, to support future combat aircraft operations. Defence should assess fuel and EO requirements for forward air bases during high tempo air operations and identify potential risks, deficiencies and mitigation measures, as part of strategic logistics assessments. To mitigate risks associated with increasing strike capabilities in the Asia-Pacific region, Defence should consider options for hardening

and resilience improvements at forward main bases and bare bases including: physical hardening, dispersal and deception measures; emerging priorities such as electro-magnetic resilience; and force structure enhancements such as increased airfield repair capability. Government should ensure that Williamtown is protected from encroachment, in view of its strategic importance in generating air combat capability."[75]

The CVW, like the CSG, would also likely be dispersed across the region. While the F/A-18C/F and Helo units would likely remain at RAAF Amberly or Williamtown with their RAAF counterparts, the E-2C, EA-6B, and C-2 assets could be based elsewhere if required. Tengah Air Base in Singapore, where the Sing Air Force is currently phasing out its aging E-2C fleet, Anderson Air Force Base in Guam, or the recently revitalized Clark International Airport (former US Air Base), and New Zealand Air Base Auckland, where their P-3 is located, represent feasible alternatives. But, as stated in the FPR, numerous airfields in Australia are being expanded and represent equally realistic options.

FBW's large capacity[76] and CVN-suitability investigation, and the fact that "55% of Australians favor allowing the U.S. to base military forces in AUS[77]" make it, from a U.S. perspective, a genuine possibility. That level of positive public reception along with a physically capable harbor, elsewhere in the *IP*, would certainly be a challenge to find.

Framework

With both the tools in hand (the integration pieces of the ANZUS naval and air forces) and the lots picked out (*FBW, FBE,* Guam, and Devonport), it is now necessary to build this new force tailored specifically to meet the concerns of the *IP* at a shared price and draw up a force-structure framework.

In addition to the CVN, a "nominal" CSG requires "four air/missile defense capable surface combatants," of which three are TLAM and Harpoon-capable (surface cruise missile)[78]. This amounts to one *Aegis*-equipped Cruiser (CG), a Destroyer Squadron (DESRON) mix of three Destroyers (DDGs) or Frigates (FFGs), a submarine (SSN), and a dedicated logistical supply ship and oiler (AOR). The CVW includes two F/A-18E/F and two F/A-18C squadrons totaling 44 strike-fighters, an Electronic-Attack squadron of four EA-6Bs, an Early Warning squadron of four E-2Cs, a logistical C-2A detachment with two aircraft, and a helicopter sea combat squadron with 19 MH-60R/S helicopters squadrons dispersed amongst the CVN and individual DESRON ships. This massive footprint roughly amounts to a CVN, four surface combatants, a submarine, logistical ship, over 60 aircraft, and approximately 7,500 personnel.

Reducing this footprint with RAN and RNZN assets and leadership would be both necessary and beneficial. RAN *Hobart* and RAN / RNZN *Anzac*-class FFGs and their attached MH-60R and SH-2G helicopters are feasible additions. Their multipurpose capabilities would make their commanders eligible for Air Defense, Anti-Submarine (USW), and Anti-Surface (SUW) roles and the established confidence in RAN commanders would justify their ownership of O-6 level (Captain) component commander roles inherent in CSG command structure. A realistic force structure proposed here would be three USN surface ships (CVN, CG, DDG,), two RAN ships (one AWD and one FFG), one RNZN FFG, and a rotation of logistical ships from each navy. RAN and RNZN P-3/P-8A maritime aircraft would be a relatively easy addition, supporting from land bases, and the soon-to-be acquired RAAF KC-30 would also be an added benefit to supporting CVW flight operations by providing airborne fuel from land bases outlined in the FPR.[79] The most complicated addition would be the RAN MH-60R and RAAF F/A-18F squadrons onboard the CVN as part of the CVW. Training of aircrew and maintenance personnel would be challenging, as CVN flight-deck operations are a fine and dangerous art. Challenges aside, given RAAF and RAN ownership of 24 MH-60R and 24 F/A-18F respectively, a theoretical CVW contribution of one helicopter squadron of 8 helicopters and one strike-fighter squadron of 10 F/A-18F is a realistic starting point.

ANZUS CTF Command structure would be similar to that of the USS Roosevelt CSG attached to the Spanish *Alvaro de Bazan*. The most likely command structure would be an *integrated*[80] one, with operational control of the *ANZUS CTF* under PACOM, administrative manning control of 7th Fleet, and the tactical control under the CSG Commander (theoretically rotated between the RAN and USN), and administrative control retained by each ANZUS military.

Counter Arguments

An opposing collective viewpoint could be that current ANZUS strategic posture and plans are correctly balanced and accurately measured, that a multinational force like this would leave the US vulnerable and damage relations with the PRC, and that establishing a feasible, effective ROE would be impossible. Admiral Greenert says that the USN will "continue robust rotational deployments to the western Pacific, complemented with our forward-stationed Navy and Marine forces in Japan, Guam, Singapore, and Australia (and) maintain rotational deployments in the Middle East and Indian Ocean. In 2025 those forces— along with our forward-stationed patrol boats, minesweepers, and littoral combat ships—will deter aggression in the region."[81] He asserts that technological advances and a continued increase in partnerships with smaller *IP* navies to be more economical, feasible, and effective. He also advocates using "Payloads" over "Platforms" and "Places" vice "Bases" in order to adequately posture the USN forward through 2025. In other words, the USN is better served by forward-deploying smaller units in order to counter piracy, using cutting-edge technology for intelligence and information dominance in order to counter terrorism and fight the global war on terror, and maintaining the status quo for CSG's deployments in order to continue operating *forward*. These lines of effort are then augmented by increasing ways in which the US military can temporally stage for future operations, cooperating with allied militaries, and greater concentration proliferation of "smart" systems.

This strategy is compelling, for collective CMF operations are countering piracy in the Horn of Africa and the Strait of Hormuz remains open today. In the Strait of Malacca, security has increased, piracy has declined, and this can be largely attested to small-scale international cooperative efforts like the Proliferation Security Initiative (PSI) and

MALSINDO (Malaysia – Singapore – Indonesia). One could surmise that when combined with MSO-tailored forces such as MALSINDO and the CMF, the addition of smaller, smarter, and faster LCS's and DDG's, will only bolster this trend. Enhanced training exercises like Cooperation Afloat Readiness & Training (CARAT) and the Southeast Asian Cooperation and Training (SEACAT) instill further confidence in the status quo. With respect to CSG's, several successful examples of mentioned previously came from continentally-based CSGs. This suggests the planned strategic posturing of FDNF's is an accurate, effective solution, and that a second forward-deployed CSG is NOT the 'end-all-be-all' for an adequate, persistent maritime presence.

A second argument against the *ANZUS-CTF* is that it makes U.S. forces *more* vulnerable, vice less, as they are now dependent on and subject to the will of AUS and NZ. What if crisis arose in Indonesia and the U.S. elected to respond in a manner similar to OIF? If AUS or NZ objected outright and pulled their forces out whilst the ANZUS CTF was underway, what becomes of those USN units thrown now into action under-equipped and thrust into combat? Additionally, moving a second CSG into the region could be akin to the ANZUS treaty itself: a Cold War-era relic of 1960's deterrence, and be seen politically as creating conditions which would damage PRC relations for decades. This is a something ANZUS would like to avoid, for the PRC could use the ANZUS-CTF as justification for aggressive, even opposing stances towards its approach to each part of the global *DIME* (Diplomacy, Information, Military, and Economic) framework.

For example, formation of the *ANZUS-CTF* could lead to a breakdown of *diplomacy* and see the PRC target other *IP* nations through *information* about an impending Anglo-Hegemonic alliance and an anti-Islamic *IP* force. This, in turn, could ignite a *military* arms race in the *IP*, and the PRC could force ANZUS to bankrupt themselves while simultaneously it pulled its *economic* purse strings in foreign investment and trade, propping itself up as THE economic superpower. Former President Dwight D. Eisenhower's fear of the *out-of-control* military machine and arms buildup could happen in the 21st century at unprecedented levels. Thus, a better approach would be détente, or rather…a smaller military presence to ease relations and increase cooperation, vice deterrence, which could lead to a second Cold War with the PRC.

Finally, coalition task forces require a high degree of trust by each participating nation, and the multinational nature of the *ANZUS-CTF* could render it ineffective as each country would be bound to depend on the will and fortitude of its partners. While MSO, HA/DR, and NATO missions would likely have bridged approval from both AUS and NZ, the CSG, at its heart, is a massive combat-ready force designed to dissuade adversaries merely through its presence and, if required defeating them via overwhelming armed force. The fragile nature and challenges of the *IP* give credence to the conviction that war-fighting *will* happen in the coming decades *somewhere* in the *IP*. When this happens, each nation will have its own view and participate or object accordingly. Differences in ROE, Diplomacy, and Law will hinder any multi-national force.

Response and Recommendations

Admiral Greenert's arguments in favor the USN's future plans and CSG status quo, the issue of vulnerability, the use of détente vice deterrence, and the complications with multinational ROE are justifiable given U.S. strategic guidance to win one war while simultaneously denying an opponent victory in another. But they are partially based on a snapshot of current conditions, things known, and a slippery-slope theory on a road to failure.

With respect to the use of forward-deployed LCSs for MSO in critical chokepoints; even when combined with multinational navies such as MALSINDO or the CMF, those units do not have the operational combat reach or capabilities of a CSG. They are tailored for a specific "mission" in specific "places", and lack the large-scale flexibility and credibility of a multi-national CSG. They would be unable to provide on-call HA/DR, deterrence, and large-scale striking power that the CSG provides. Put bluntly, a small and fast 'brains over brawn' approach only goes so far. The *IP* is a big "place"…and merits a large force.

In responding to the "détente" over "deterrence" approach towards the PRC, this could be accomplished through greater *diplomatic* engagement from each ANZUS country, but also requires the PRC to do the same. However, ANZUS nations are realistic, aligned, and most importantly…correct, in their assessments of the PRC and its *growing influence* within the *IP*. While this subject ventures beyond the operational realm and into the strategic, the PRC poses a dicey, diplomatic problem that requires a strong operational solution. The "Walk Softly but carry a Big Stick" approach of former President Theodore

Roosevelt; fitting words from the creator of the aforementioned Great White Fleet, applies here. "T.R." would stand and applaud the formation of the *ANZUS-CTF.*

Finally, the problem in ROE can be summed in the following assertion: *ROE is a challenge for any multinational force, but if it could work anywhere, this would be it.* Because ANZUS nations are aligned; from military capabilities and strategies to the shared history of its people, and diplomatically aligned governments provides a retort to the '*it could never work'* naysayers, the ANZUS-CTF really does benefit each nation on relatively equal levels while also benefitting the region as a whole. Put simply, it provides assurance to allies and relief to those who would require it.

For the U.S., an increase in CSG FDNF's dramatically increases strategic options. The complex problem of the environment, the *time-space-force* factors affecting current CSG positioning, and rising costs would ALL be addressed with both a geographic and consolidated footprint. AUS and NZ would greatly benefit by bridging strategic and capability gaps while simultaneously increasing their own defenses and combat credibility. This marked increase would allow defense budgets to be tailored to further expand the defenses of each ANZUS partner. At once, two trusted U.S. Allies within the *IP* could claim a CSG as part of their arsenal while the U.S. would gain increased access and presence in the region. For ANZUS, operating under a multi-national banner would ease any unwanted regional perception of a unilateral US approach while providing greater MSO support and HA/DR goodwill assurance to struggling IP partners. Strategically allied nations, from Japan to Saudi Arabia, would see that the U.S. is firmly committed to *IP* stability despite economic difficulties. Iran and DPRK intentions could be deterred and PRC expansion checked.

Conclusion

If global fortunes took a turn for the worse, current and future forward-deployed USN posturing would be inadequate and the security of the *IP* would be compromised. What if PRC encroachment overtook Taiwan and Iran seized the opportunity to close the Strait of Hormuz? What if the DPRK initiated attacked South Korea after a tsunami ravaged Southeast Asia? What if terrorist exploded a dirty bomb in the Straits of Malacca after a commercial oil tanker ran aground exiting the Suez Canal, leading to a massive oil slick and massive disruption in global commerce? Even worse, what if three of these happened around the same time?

If these horrible, yet possible circumstances did unfold, the *international* community would thankfully look to the southwestern shore of Australia for a rapid response and take solace in an approaching multinational-flagged CSG. The ANZUS relationship, naval history, shared challenges, aligned strategies, and genuine opportunity at Perth; together, are *ample* reasons to make-ready *Fleet Base West* and increase *IP* maritime presence with the ***ANZUS Carrier Task Force.***

NOTES

[1] Admiral John Greenert, USN, *20th International Sea Power Symposium*. United States Naval War College, Newport, RI, October 19, 2011.

[2] Bruce Vaughn, "Australia: Background and U.S. Relations," *Congressional Research Service,* January 13, 2012. http://www.fas.org/sgp/crs/row/RL33010.pdf/.

[3] Bruce Vaughn, "New Zealand: Background and Bilateral Relations with the United States," *Congressional Research Service*, May 27, 2011. http://www.fas.org/sgp/crs/row/RL32876.pdf/.

[4] Greenert, *20th International Seapower Symposium.*

[5] Humanitarian Assistance to Combat Operations: The full spectrum capability of aircraft carriers" November 1, 2011, http://cjoscoe.org/published_docs.html.

[6] Greenert, *20th International Seapower Symposium.*

[7] Barak Obama, POTUS, to the Australian Parliament, *An Address.* November 17, 2011 http://www.whitehouse.gov/the-press-office/2011/11/17/remarks-president-obama-australian-parliament.

[8] Mark E. Manyin et al, "Pivot to the Pacific? The Obama Administration's "Rebalancing" Toward Asia," *Congressional Research Service*, March 28, 2012. http://www.fas.org/sgp/crs/natsec/R42448.pdf

[9] United States Navy, *Naval Operations Concept 2010: Implementing the Maritime Strategy,* (Washington, DC: GPO, 2010). www.navy.mil/maritime/noc.

[10] United States Energy Information Administration, *Country Analysis Brief: World Oil Transit Chokepoints,* (Washington, DC: GPO, Dec 30, 2011). www.eia.doe.gov.

[11] Admiral John Greenert, USN, *Testimony before the Congress on the FY2013 Department of Navy Posture.* March 2012

[12] Vaughn, "Australia: Background and U.S. Relations."

[13] Ronald O'Rourke, "China Naval Modernization: Implications for U.S. Navy Capabilities - Background and Issues for Congress," *Congressional Research Service*, August 26, 2010

[14] "How Old is Australia's Navy? SEMAPHORE, Pub 2. 2002," Royal Australian Navy, accessed on April 25, 2012, http://www.navy.gov.au/Publication:Semaphore_-_Issue_2,_2002.

[15] "The Battle of the Coral Sea," Royal Australian Navy, accessed on April 25, 2012, http://www.navy.gov.au/Battle_of_the_Coral_Sea.

[16] "SEATO EXERCISE SEA DEVIL," Royal Australian Navy, accessed on April 25 2012, 2012, http://www.navy.gov.au/SEATO_Exercise_Sea_Devil.

[17] "History of the RAN," Royal Australian Navy, accessed on April 25, 2012, http://www.navy.gov.au/history.

[18] "Operation Slipper," Royal Australian Navy, accessed on April 25, 2012, http://www.navy.gov.au/Operation_Slipper#Maritime_Operations.

[19] "Australia Assumes Command of Combined Task Force 150," Combined Maritime Forces, last modified on December 16, 2011, http://combinedmaritimeforces.com.

[20] "Talsiman Sabre 2011," Royal Australian Navy, accessed on April 25, 2012, http://www.navy.gov.au/Talisman_Sabre_2011.

[21] "A vision of Navy's Amphibious Future," Royal Australian Navy, last modified on September 17, 2010, http://www.navy.gov.au/A_Vision_of_Navy's_Amphibious_Future.

[22] Neil Howard, "75 Years of the New Zealand Navy," *Friends of the Hocken and the Hocken Library Staff,* no 17, last modified in August 1996 http://www.library.otago.ac.nz/pdf/hoc_fr_bulletins/17_bulletin.pdf.

[23] Ibid.

[24] A. Young, "NZ Navy to Join US-Led Exercise," *New Zealand Herald,* April 4, 2011.

[25] Vaughn, "New Zealand: Background and Bilateral Relations with the United States."

[26] "Pacific Partnership 2011", Royal Australian Navy, accessed on April 25, 2012, http://www.navy.gov.au/Pacific_Partnership_2011.

[27] Vaughn, "New Zealand: Background and Bilateral Relations with the United States."

[28] U.S. Department of Defense. *Secretary of Defense Leon E. Panetta, Statement on Fiscal Budget 2013*, (Washington, DC: GPO January 26, 2012).

[29] Manyin, "Pivot to the Pacific? The Obama Administration's "Rebalancing" Toward Asia," March 28, 2012.

[30] Hillary Clinton, "America's Pacific Century," *Foreign Policy*, November 2011, www.foreignpolicy.com/articles/2011/10/11/americas_pacific_century.

[31] Vaughn, "Australia: Background and U.S. Relations," January 13, 2012.

[32] Australian Government, Department of Defence, *Defending Australia in the Asia Pacific Century: Force 2030 Defence White Paper 2009* (Canberra, Australia: GPO 2009), http://www.defence.gov/aus.

[33] Vaughn, "Australia: Background and U.S. Relations."

[34] U.S. Department of State, *U.S.-Australia Ministerial Consultations 2011 Joint Statement*, (Washington, DC: GPO November 8, 2010).

[35] U.S. Department of State, *Prime Minister of Australia, President of the United States, "Australia-United States Force Posture Initiatives,* (Washington, DC: GPO November 16, 2011).

[36] U.S. Department of State, *U.S.-Australia Ministerial Consultations 2011 Joint Statement*, (Washington, DC: GPO September 15, 2011).

[37] U.S. Department of Defense, *Sustaining U.S. Global Leadership: Priorities for 21st Century Defense,* (Washington, DC: GPO January 2012), www.defense.gov/news/Defense_Strategic_Guidance.pdf.

[38] New Zealand Government, Department of Defence, *Defence White Paper 2010*, (Wellington, NZ: GPO 2010), www.defence.govt.nz.

[39] Ibid.

[40] Ibid.

[41] NATO, Commander, Joint Operations Staff, *Humanitarian Assistance to Combat Operations: The Full Spectrum Capabilities of Aircraft Carriers,* (NATO: GPO 2011) last modified February 1, 2011, https://transnet.act.nato.int/WISE/COE/Individual/CJOS/PublishedP/FullSpectr/file/_WFS/Full%20Spectrum%20Capability%20of%20Aircraft%20Carriers.pdf.

[42] Ryan Valverde, "BHR's HC·ll Det. Rescues Trapped Indonesian Tsunami Victims," *U.S. Navy Public Affairs,* last modified January 2005, www.navy.mil.

[43] US Southern Command Public Affairs, "Aircraft Carrier Carl Vinson Completes Haiti Relief Efforts," last modified on February 1, 2010, http://www.navy.mil/search/display.asp?story_id=50991

[44] Ryan Zielonka, "Chronology of Operation Tomodachi: Amidst Trial, Ties That Bind: Enduring Strength in the U.S.-Japan Alliance," *National Bureau of Asian Affairs*, accessed on April 25, 2012, http://www.nbr.org/research/activity.aspx?id=121.

[45] Ben Lambert, "Operation Enduring Freedom: An Assessment," RAND, last modified 2005, http://www.rand.org/content/dam/rand/pubs/research_briefs/2005/RAND_RB9148.pdf.

[46] E.D. McGrady and Robert E. Sullivan, "Operation Uphold Democracy; Observations on Joint Assault Forces Operated From a CV," *Center for Naval Analyses*, July 1996. http://www.cna.org/research/1996/operation-uphold-democracy-observations-joint.

[47] Go Navy. CV Positions, last modified May 2, 2012, http://www.gonavy.jp/CVLocation.html.

[48] US Navy Public Affairs, "About COMCARSTRKGRU FIVE", Accessed on April 25, 2012. Available at http://www.public.navy.mil/surfor/ccsg5/Pages/ourship.aspx

[49] O'Rourke, Ronald. "China Naval Modernization: Implications for U.S. Navy Capabilities— Background and Issues for Congress." *Congressional Research Service*. August 26, 2010.

[50] *The Economist Online,* "Chinese missile ranges: China's missiles," December 6, 2010. Available at http://www.economist.com/blogs/dailychart/2010/12/chinese_missile_ranges&fsrc=nwl.

[51] U.S. Department of Defense , *"ANNUAL REPORT TO CONGRESS: Military and Security Developments Involving the People's Republic of China"* (Washington, DC: GPO January 2011).

[52] Ibid.

[53] Ibid.

[54] Australian Government, Department of Defence, *Defending Australia in the Asia Pacific Century: Force 2030 Defence White Paper 2009.*

[55] Ibid.

[56] Australian Government, Department of Defence, *Australian Defence Force Posture Review Progress Report,* (Canberra, Australia: GPO, January 2012), http://www.defence.gov.au/oscdf/adf-posture-review/.

[57] Royal Australian Navy, "Hobart Class," http://www.navy.gov.au/Hobart_Class, Accessed April 25, 2012

[58] Australian Government, Department of Defence, *Defending Australia in the Asia Pacific Century: Force 2030 Defence White Paper 2009.*

[59] New Zealand Government, *Statement of Intent 2011 – 2014, New Zealand Defence Force,* (Wellington, NZ: GPO January 2011)

[60] Royal Australian Navy, "Purchase of offshore support vessel for Humanitarian Assistance and Disaster Relief, 19 March 2012, Accessed at http://www.navy.gov.au/Purchase_of_Offshore_Support_Vessel_for_Humanitarian_and_Disaster_Relief

[61] Patrick Gower, "Navy ships project hard to keep afloat," Dec 11, 2008 Accessed at http://www.nzherald.co.nz/royal-nz-navy/news/article.cfm?o_id=439&objectid=10547518

[62] New Zealand Government, *Statement of Intent 2011 – 2014, New Zealand Defence Force*

[63] Kimberly Stephens, "Spanish Ship Joins TR Strike Group" USS Theodore Roosevelt Public Affairs. Last modified on May 6, 2005. Available at http://www.navy.mil/search/display.asp?story_id=18207.

[64] Royal Australian Navy, "Navy Annual 2007, HMAS Melbourne." Accessed on April 25, 2012. Available at http://www.navy.gov.au/Publication:Navy_Annual_2007/HMAS_Melbourne

[65] Candice Kauta and Rialyn Rodrigo, "Cross-Deck to ABE LINCOLN," Royal New Zealand Navy, last modified on July 30, 2008, http://www.navy.mil.nz/know-your-navy/official-documents/navy-today/nt08webformat/sep08/abe-lincoln.htm.

[66] Philip Carder, "Backgrounder: F/A-18E/F Super Hornet,", The Boeing Corporation. Last modified in April 2012, http://www.boeing.com/defense-space/military/fa18ef/docs/EF_overview.pdf.

[67] Mark Dodd, "Carrier training for our pilots," *The Australian*, Last modified on August 21, 2007, http://www.theaustralian.com.au/national-affairs/defence/carrier-training-for-our-pilots/story-e6frg8yo-1111114230336

[68] Eli Manuel, "Ship Integration - a Prerequisite for New Navy Helicopters," *Air Power Australia Analysis*, Last modified on May 16, 2007, http://www.ausairpower.net/APA-2007-03.html.

[69] U.S. Department of State, *"Secretary of State Hillary Clinton Remarks With Australian Foreign Minister Robert Carr After Their Meeting,"* (Washington, DC: GPO, April 24, 2012), http://www.state.gov/secretary/rm/2012/04/188428.htm.

[70] Manyin, "Pivot to the Pacific? The Obama Administration's "Rebalancing" Toward Asia."

[71] Ibid.

[72] Ibid.

[73] Australian Government, Department of Defence, *Australian Defence Force Posture Review Progress Report.*

[74] Ibid.

[75] Australian Government, Department of Defence. Australian Defence Force Posture Review. Canberra, Australia: GPO, March 30 2012.

[76] Royal Australian Navy, "HMAS Stirling," Accessed on April 25, 2012. Available at http://www.navy.gov.au/HMAS_Stirling

[77] Fergus Hanson, "2011 Lowy Institute Poll," http://www.lowyinterpreter.org

[78] U.S. Department of the Navy, "OPNAVINST 3501.316B - Policy for baseline composition and basic mission capabilities for major afloat navy and naval groups ,"(Washington, DC: GPO October 21, 2010).

[79] Australian Government, Department of Defence. *Australian Defence Force Posture Review.* Canberra, Australia: GPO, March 30 2012.

[80] U.S. Department of Defense, "Joint Publication 3-16: Multinational Operations," (Washington, DC: GPO March 7, 2007).

[81] Adm John W. Greenert, 2011 "Navy 2025: Forward Warfighters," *Proceedings*, 137, no. 12.

BIBLIOGRAPHY

Australian Government, Department of Defence. *Australian Defence Force Posture Review.* Canberra, Australia: GPO, March 30 2012.

Australian Government, Department of Defence. *Australian Defence Force Posture Review Progress Report.* Canberra, Australia: GPO, January 2012.

--- Department of Defence. *Defending Australia in the Asia Pacific Century: Force 2030 Defence White Paper 2009.* Canberra, Australia: GPO, 2009.

Carder, Philip. "Backgrounder: F/A-18E/F Super Hornet." The Boeing Corporation. Last modified April 2012. www.boeing.com/defensespace/military/fa18ef/docs/EF_overview.pdf.

Clinton, Hillary. "America's Pacific Century," *Foreign Policy*, November 2011, www.foreignpolicy.com/articles/2011/10/11/americas_pacific_century.

Combined Maritime Forces. "Combined Maritime Forces: Australia Assumes Command of Combined Task Force 150." December 16, 2011. http://combinedmaritimeforces.com.

Dodd, Mark. "Carrier training for our pilots." *The Australian*, August 21, 2007. www.theaustralian.com.au/national-affairs/defence/carrier- training-for-our -pilots/story-e6frg8yo-1111114230336.

Go Navy. CV Positions. Last modified May 2, 2012. http://www.gonavy.jp/CVLocation.html.

Gower, Patrick. "Navy ships project hard to keep afloat." *New Zealand Herald.* Dec 11, 2008.

Greenert, John W. "Navy 2025: Forward Warfighters" *Proceedings* 137, no. 12. 2011.

--- *20th International Sea Power Symposium.* United States Naval War College, Newport, RI, October 19, 2011.

--- *Testimony before the Congress on the FY2013 Department of Navy Posture.* U.S. Senate, Washington D.C., March 2012.

Hanson, Fergus. "2011 Lowy Institute Poll," *Lowly Institute for International Policy.* 2011. http://www.lowyinterpreter.org

Howard, Neil. "75 Years of the New Zealand Navy." *Hocken Library*, no 17. (August 1996): www.library.otago.ac.nz/pdf/hoc_fr_bulletins/17_bulletin.pdf.

Kauta, Candice and Rialyn Rodrigo, "Cross-Deck to ABE LINCOLN." *Royal New Zealand Navy*. July 30, 2008. www.navy.mil.nz/know-your-navy/official-k documents/navytoday/nt08webformat/sep08/abe-lincoln.htm.

Lambert, Ben "Operation Enduring Freedom: An Assessment," RAND. Last modified 2005. www.rand.org/content/dam/rand/pubs/research_briefs/2005/RAND_RB9148.pdf.

Manuel, Eli. "Ship Integration - a Prerequisite for New Navy Helicopters." *Air Power Australia Analysis,* May 16, 2007. www.ausairpower.net/APA-2007-03.html.

Manyin, Mark E. "Pivot to the Pacific? The Obama Administration's "Rebalancing" Toward Asia." *Congressional Research Service.* March 28, 2012.

McGrady, E.D. and Robert E. Sullivan. "Operation Uphold Democracy; Observations on Joint Assault Forces Operated From a CV." *Center for Naval Analyses*, July 1996. www.cna.org/research/1996/operation-uphold-democracy-observations-joint.

NATO Commander, Joint Operations Staff. "Humanitarian Assistance to Combat Operations: The full spectrum capability of aircraft carriers." November 1, 2011.

New Zealand Government, Department of Defence. *Defence White Paper 2010.* Wellington, NZ: 2010.

--- *Statement of Intent 2011 – 2014, New Zealand Defence Force.* Wellington, NZ: January 2011.

O'Rourke, Ronald. "China Naval Modernization: Implications for U.S. Navy Capabilities— Background and Issues for Congress." *Congressional Research Service.* August 26, 2010.

Royal Australian Navy. "A vision of Navy's Amphibious Future." www.navy.gov.au/A_Vision_of_Navy's_Amphibious_Future

--- "Battle of the Coral Sea." www.navy.gov.au/Battle_of_the_Coral_Sea.

--- "How Old is Australia's Navy?" www.navy.gov.au/Publication:Semaphore_-_Issue_2,_2002.

--- "History of the RAN." www.navy.gov.au/history

--- "HMAS Stirling." http://www.navy.gov.au/HMAS_Stirling

--- "Hobart Class." www.navy.gov.au/Hobart_Class

--- "Navy Annual 2007, HMAS Melbourne."
www.navy.gov.au/Publication:Navy_Annual_2007/HMAS_Melbourne

--- "Operation Slipper." www.navy.gov.au/Operation_Slipper#Maritime_Operations.

--- "Pacific Partnership 2011." www.navy.gov.au/Pacific_Partnership_2011

--- "Purchase of offshore support vessel for Humanitarian Assistance and Disaster Relief." 19 March 2012, www.navy.gov.au.

--- "SEATO EXERCISE SEA DEVIL." www.navy.gov.au/SEATO_Exercise_Sea_Devil.

--- "Talisman Sabre 2011." www.navy.gov.au/Talisman_Sabre_2011

Stephens, Kimberly. "Spanish Ship Joins TR Strike Group" *USS Theodore Roosevelt Public Affairs.* www.navy.mil/search/display.asp?story_id=18207.

The Economist Online, "Chinese missile ranges: China's missiles," December 6, 2010. http://www.economist.com/blogs/dailychart/2010/12/chinese_missile_ranges&fsrc=nwl.

U.S. Department of Defense. *Joint Publication 3-16: Multinational Operations.* GPO: March 7, 2007.

--- *Secretary of Defense Leon E. Panetta. Statement on Fiscal Budget 2013.* GPO: January 26, 2012.

--- *Sustaining U.S. Global Leadership: Priorities for 21st Century Defense.* GPO: January 2012.

--- *"ANNUAL REPORT TO CONGRESS: Military and Security Developments Involving the People's Republic of China"* Washington, DC: GPO January 2011.

U.S. Department of State. "Remarks by President Obama to the Australian Parliament." Parliament House, Canberra, Australia. GPO: November 17, 2011.

--- *Prime Minister of Australia, President of the United States, Australia-United States Force Posture Initiatives.* Washington, DC: GPO, November 16, 2011.

--- *Secretary of State Hillary Clinton, Remarks With Australian Foreign Minister Robert Carr After Their Meeting.* Washington, DC: GPO, April 24, 2012.

--- *U.S.-Australia Ministerial Consultations 2011 Joint Statement." AUSMIN 2010.* Canberra, Australia: GPO, November 8, 2010.

--- *U.S.-Australia Ministerial Consultations 2011 Joint Statement."AUSMIN 2011.* San Francisco, CA: GPO, September 15, 2011.

U.S. Energy Information Administration. *Country Analysis Brief: World Oil Transit Chokepoints.* Washington DC: GPO: Dec 30, 2011.

U.S. Navy. *Naval Operations Concept 2010: Implementing the Maritime Strategy.* Washington DC: GPO, 2010.

--- "OPNAVINST 3501.316B - Policy for baseline composition and basic mission capabilities for major afloat navy and naval groups ," Washington DC: GPO October 21, 2010.

--- "About COMCARSTRKGRU FIVE." www.public.navy.mil/surfor/ccsg5/Pages/ourship.aspx

U.S. Southern Command Public Affairs, "Aircraft Carrier Carl Vinson Completes Haiti Relief Efforts," February 1, 2011 www.navy.mil/search/display.asp?story_id=50991

Valverde, Ryan. "BHR's HC·ll Det. Rescues Trapped Indonesian Tsunami Victims," *U.S. Navy Public Affairs Office,* January 2005. www.navy.mil.

Vaughn, Bruce "Australia: Background and U.S. Relations," *Congressional Research Service.* January 13, 2012.

--- "New Zealand: Background and Bilateral Relations with the United States," *Congressional Research Service.* May 27, 2011.

Young, Audrey. "NZ Navy to Join US-Led Exercise," *The New Zealand Herald*, April 4, 2011.

Zielonka, Ryan. "Chronology of Operation Tomodachi: Amidst Trial, Ties That Bind: Enduring Strength in the U.S.-Japan Alliance." *National Bureau of Asian Affairs*, www.nbr.org/research/activity.aspx?id=121